CHINESE NEW YEAR

Sarah Moyse

WAYLAND

CARNIVAL

ID-UL-FITR

CHRISTMAS

DIWALI

PASSOVER

Editors: Sarah Doughty/Jannet King
Designer: Tim Mayer

First published in 1996 by Wayland Publishers Ltd
61 Western Road, Hove, East Sussex BN3 1JD

British Library Cataloguing in Publication Data
Moyse, Sarah
    Chinese New Year. – (Festivals)
    1. Chinese New Year – Juvenile literature
    I.Title
    394.2'683

ISBN 0 7502 1939 4

Printed and bound by L.E.G.O S.p.A, Italy.

Picture acknowledgements
Circa cover bottom left, 8, 13 top (John Smith), 17, 22-3 top; Eye Ubiquitous 11, 16 (Julia Waterlow), 29 right (P.M Field); Robert Harding cover bottom right (R Ian Lloyd), cover centre, 4 bottom right (Corrigan), 6 (Adam Woolfitt), 19 top, 26 (Adam Woolfitt), 27 top (Jeremy Nicholl); Impact 4 middle top (Jeremy Nicholl), 4 far right and 25 (Christophe Bluntzer), 4 middle bottom (Alain Evrard), 27 top (Jeremy Nicholl), 28 (Alain Evrard); Occidor (Gina Corrigan) 5 left, 23 bottom; Panos 12 (Wang Gang Feng), 20 (Trevor Page); Hong Kong Tourist Board 10, 7 bottom, 14, 21 top, 22 bottom; Topham Picturepoint cover top right, 4 far left, 5 bottom right, 24; Trip 7 top (Moscrop), 13 bottom (R.Vargas), 15 bottom (H.Rogers), 21 bottom (F.Good); Wayland Picture Library 29 (left); Zefa 5 top, 15 top. Border artwork by Tim Mayer; artwork by Linden Artists; calligraphy by Erica Burt.

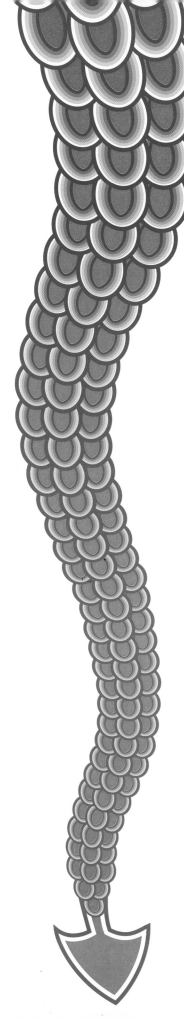

CONTENTS

CHINESE NEW YEAR AROUND THE WORLD

A traditional Chinese Dragon winds its way through the streets of Turfan in the Xinjiang Province.

New Year is celebrated with great enthusiasm in London's Soho – one of the centres of the Chinese-speaking community in Britain.

A temple in Rangoon, Burma, showing people bringing offerings to the gods and lighting incense at Chinese New Year. They hope that their offerings and prayers will ensure harmony with the gods and bring good fortune in the coming year.

These colourful floats form part of the Singapore Annual Chingay Parade. Lanterns of all imaginable shapes and sizes are displayed.

These farmers dress up as very fat people with big heads. This is because fatness implies a person is well-fed and everyone hopes that their crops will grow well in the New Year.

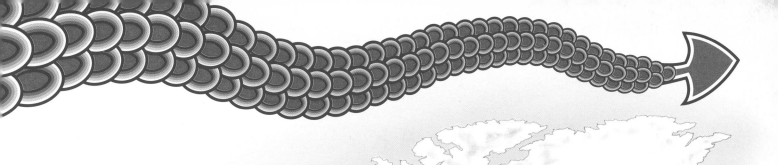

Street celebrations in Vancouver, Canada outside the China Gate. The Chinese Lion is dancing for offerings of greens and money in red envelopes attached to the shop sign dangling in the foreground.

Stilt walking is a favourite entertainment at New Year. There are many different types of stilt displays, some highly energetic, some, like these stilt walkers, calm and beautiful. The name, Yangge or seedling song, comes from the songs sung by peasants planting rice seedlings. These performers from the Heilongjiang Province, China, dress up as characters from traditional stories.

A street celebration in Washington DC with their Dragon ready to go into action.

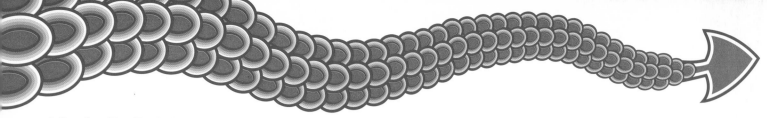

HAPPY NEW YEAR

The Lunar New Year is the most important festival of the Chinese year. It is the celebration to welcome the start of a new year and a festival of family reunion. Families who live apart come together to celebrate. Although outside the Chinese-speaking world (China, Taiwan, Singapore, and some parts of Malaysia) Chinese New Year is not a public holiday, families still celebrate with a family get-together and a special meal, either on Chinese New Year's Eve or on the first weekend after the Chinese New Year.

Above: A Chinese Dragon, tempted with a 'pearl' and a fire stick, dances through the streets of Singapore.

FIRECRACKERS

Firecrackers were traditionally let off to frighten away ghosts so that the new year would be free of them. Legend says that long ago there was a monster who terrorised people and animals at the end of the year. It was discovered that this animal was frightened of loud noises, bright lights and the colour red. At midnight, on the last day of the old year, these things are used to chase away the monster for the whole year.

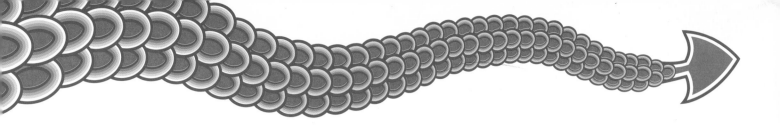

Firecrackers and fireworks are an important part of the New Year celebration. Whole market stalls are devoted to selling them.

Below: Chinese New Year is a very special time for Chinese-speaking children around the world. This child in traditional costume is holding red money envelopes. In the background are flowering plum blossom and New Year's greeting cards.

Chinese New Year is a family celebration that takes place in the home. The Chinese place particular importance on caring for the family. This is particularly true at the New Year Festival when the very young are treated specially because of their importance for the future, and the old are honoured for their connection with the past.

Public celebrations of Chinese New Year happen all over the world; cities with Chinese communities celebrate with Lion and Dragon Dances and parades with traditional costumes. They also welcome the new year with firecrackers. In China many places have traditional celebrations that last for several days.

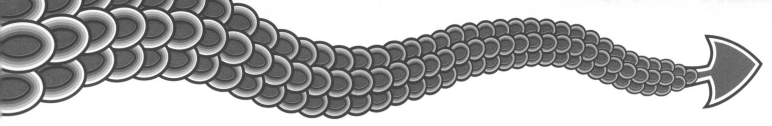

ORIGIN OF THE CELEBRATION

The start of the New Year has been celebrated in China for more than 3,000 years. New Year was a time when the farmers gave thanks for the harvest and prayed to the gods for a good harvest in the coming year. This was the one period in the busy farming year when there was time to have a celebration and when the family could get together, relax and be merry.

Chinese New Year begins with a New Moon. The Lunar Year is calculated from the time it takes for the Moon to travel round the Earth, while the Western (Gregorian) calendar is based on the time it takes for the Earth to circle the Sun. The orbits of the Moon bear no relation to the time it takes for the Earth to go round the Sun, which is why the Chinese Lunar New Year is celebrated on a different date each year. In China the New Year was renamed the Spring Festival, in 1911, when the Western calendar was officially accepted in China. However it is still commonly known around the world as the Chinese New Year.

CHINESE ALMANAC

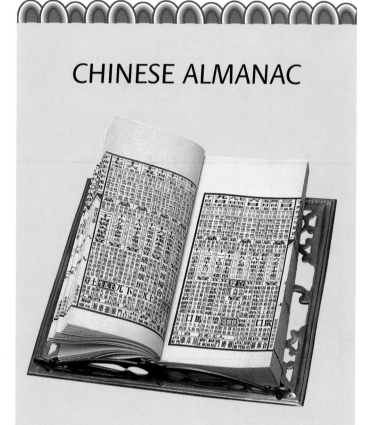

The 'Know Everything Book' (Tong Shu), or Chinese almanac, has been in publication since about 2200 BC. It tells farmers when to plant crops and gives dates of religious festivals. It lists lucky days for different activities: getting married, cutting one's hair or taking in a cat. It contains poetry, proverbs, charms and mystical signs as well as horoscopes and interpretations of dreams and symptoms such as sneezing. These almanacs are still very popular.

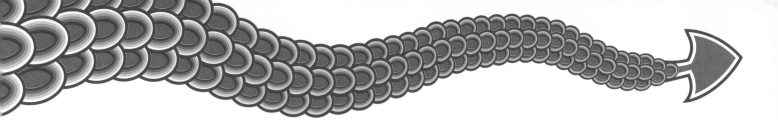

Chinese years are named after one of twelve animals. These have been used in the same order to name the years since the sixth century AD. Each animal is said to have its own personality and emotions, which are present in people born within its year.

THE 12 ANIMALS AND THEIR 'PERSONALITIES'

Rats are cheerful, charming and welcome everywhere. They crave excitement and are easily bored.

Oxen are hard-working and patient. Usually shy and self-reliant, they can be difficult.

Tigers have a forceful personality and are adventurous and confident. They can see all sides to a problem, but not the answer.

Rabbits are real home lovers and very peaceable and sociable. They are often shy and secretive.

Dragons have strong personalities. They love their freedom and hate routine. They are popular and generous, but can be inconsistent.

Snakes are sensitive with a strong sense of responsibility. They are usually charming people with a well-developed sense of humour. Sometimes they are a bit selfish and like to hoard their money.

Horses are hard-working, admirable and ambitious. Careful with money, they also like to play hard.

Rams are gentle and caring and achieve what they want by kindness. They love beautiful things and have strong family feelings.

Monkeys are charming, cheeky and clever, often with little respect for authority. They are creative and successful in most things, especially in business.

Roosters are faithful to family and friends. They are organized, punctual and hard-working. They can be arrogant, giving advice that is not asked for.

Dogs are loyal and caring with a fearless streak. They hate injustice and need to learn patience when trying to change things.

Pigs are peace-loving, trusting, strong and straightforward and like a quiet life. They make good leaders but would rather be a member of a team.

To read the Calendar, the year falls between two dates eg. Rabbit between 29 Jan 1987 and 16 Feb 1988.

RELIGIONS AND RITUALS

Although the New Year celebration is not mainly a religious one, many Chinese will visit a temple at this time of the year to make an offering to the Buddha or to the gods in the hope of making the New Year a good one. Ancestors and gods are honoured with ceremonies in the home around a family altar decorated with flowers. Incense and candles are burned at the altar.

At important family banquets the ancestors may be recognized as 'spiritual guests' and first offered food that is afterwards eaten with the meal.

Celebrating the New Year is full of rituals. This picture includes a traditional New Year greeting, with three 'immortals' from folklore, blossom, oranges (which are associated with gold), sticky cake and New Year decorations.

The Chinese have three main systems of ideas that are important to them: Confucianism, Daoism and Buddhism. Although these systems are very different, many Chinese follow some or all of the rituals associated with them just to be safe.

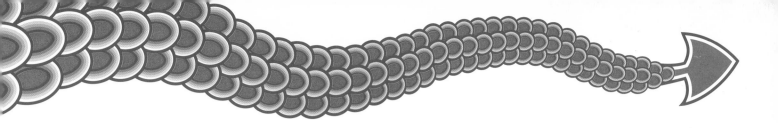

Confucius lived in the fifth century BC and spoke about the value of good behaviour in private life and in government. He said that politeness, honesty, courage and loyalty were what made good people. He believed in self-development through education and thought that people gain in wisdom as they grow older. It is part of the Confucian tradition to honour parents and ancestors.

The walls of this temple in Hohot, in Inner Mongolia are decorated with the eight trigrams around the Yin Yang (female/male, dark/light) symbol. A trigram is three lines of yin and yang. Yang is an unbroken line, yin a broken one.

Daoism comes from the teachings of Laozi, who lived at the same time as Confucius. His book, the Dao De Jing (The Way and its Power), describes the way (dao means 'way') to live at peace with nature so as not to upset natural balances. The Way involves balance between opposite forces. They are called Yin and Yang. While Yin is dark and female, Yang is the opposite, being light and male.

When Yin and Yang are balanced then there is perfect harmony with nature.

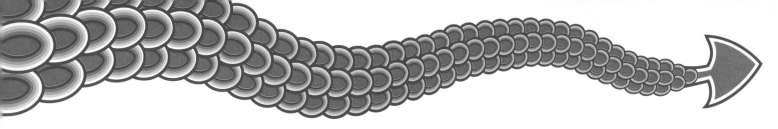

Unlike Confucianism and Daoism, which started in China, Buddhism came from India and is based on the teachings of the Buddha – a holy man. Buddha taught that people need to let go of earthly desires and become fully aware of what they are doing in the present. Buddhists believe that after death each soul moves on to another body which may be animal or human. What one is chosen for in the next life depends on how good or bad the person has been in this life.

Sukyamuni is the founder of Buddhism. He saw that all humans suffer birth, age, illness and death and that nothing in the universe is permanent. He teaches that if everyone behaves well towards everyone else then there will be peace in the universe.

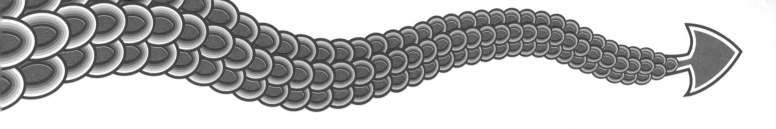

DOOR GODS

The Door Gods are two fierce warriors who frighten away evil spirits. Originally, these warriors were generals who watched over the emperor when evil spirits were tormenting him. While they guarded him the spirits left the emperor alone. The emperor discovered that the spirits were even frightened of the warriors' pictures so he had paintings of them pasted on his doors. Other people also made copies of these pictures to protect themselves and this practice continues as a tradition.

The Chinese also pray to other gods, holding the view that the more gods who can look after them the better. The important ones are the Kitchen God, who watches the family in the home, the Jade Emperor, who is the most important god in heaven, the God of Wealth, who determines how wealthy people are, and the Door Gods.

Buddhist monks are supported throughout the year by the local community. This monk from Paoan temple in Taiwan is accepting an offering.

PREPARATIONS FOR NEW YEAR

Preparations for the New Year Festival start up to a month before. Since the Qin Dynasty, over 2,000 years ago, there has been a custom of marking a day of worship three weeks before the New Year. On this day offerings were made to the family ancestors and household gods. A special food, 'Eight Precious Rice' or Laba, is traditionally eaten at this time. It consists of a sticky rice containing at least eight other ingredients that represent jewels. Lotus seeds, melon seeds, red dates, dried apricots, sweet red and yellow bean paste, almonds, walnuts, and raisins are all used.

In many parts of the Chinese-speaking world, it is customary to hold a flower fair before the New Year. Having flowers in bloom (especially blossom of the peach or plum tree) on the first day of the year is meant to bring good luck.

In the week before the new year, people spring clean. This is a time of renewal; houses are cleaned and maybe even painted to start the new year fresh and clean. This is also a time to renew friendships by sending greetings cards, and a time to exchange presents with relatives. The tradition of sending New Year cards as a greeting is said to have started 2,000 years ago, long before the tradition of sending cards in the West.

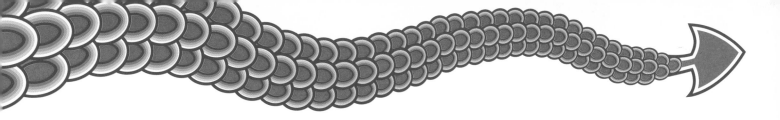

Stalls outside temples sell incense sticks, red money envelopes and New Year decorations.

People buy clothes in preparation for New Year's Day so that they have something new to wear. In ancient China the farmers would set aside days to go to market to buy cloth and other items to prepare for the new year celebrations. The preparations in countries outside of China concentrate on providing a reminder of Chinese traditions perhaps neglected during the rest of the year.

RED ENVELOPES

Presents of money are given at New Year in a red envelope with good luck characters on it – money given like this may not be refused and the pretty envelope makes the present less vulgar. The immediate family give presents to children on New Year's Eve. This is called Ya Sui Qian, meaning 'suppressing age money' which is supposed to stop the children getting older. This comes from the tradition that everyone becomes one year older on New Year's Day. Red is a lucky colour and will bring good luck to the person receiving the present.

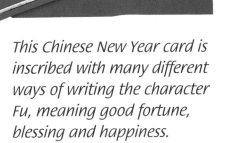

This Chinese New Year card is inscribed with many different ways of writing the character Fu, meaning good fortune, blessing and happiness.

SUPERSTITIONS AND TRADITIONS

Superstitions in Chinese culture are different from those in Western society and, although slowly dying out, people still respect them even if they do not believe them any more.

This little boy in Guangzhou Province is having a hair cut in preparation for the New Year.

The Chinese think that whatever happens on New Year's Day will shape the events of the year to come. For instance, if you are lucky in gambling, then you will be lucky for the rest of the year; if it rains, it will be a wet year, and so on.

Knives, scissors and all sharp objects are not used during the first five days of the New Year period because they may cut away luck while they are being used. Clothes and food are prepared in advance of the New Year Festival so that no work needs to be done that might require the use of a sharp tool. Hair is not cut in the new year holiday period so everyone goes for a haircut just before.

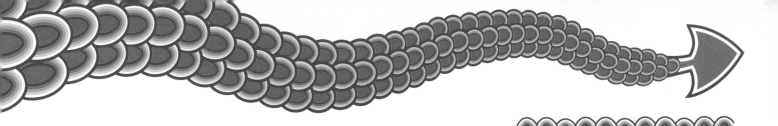

During the holiday period, no one uses bad language or words that are unlucky (such as 'die', 'owe', 'accident' or 'sick') in case they cause misfortune in the coming year. Everyone makes a big effort to be in a good mood and be happy and friendly towards everyone else. People use positive words like 'profit', 'promotion' and 'wealth'.

KITCHEN GOD

According to tradition, the Kitchen God goes to Heaven a week before the New Year to report on the family's behaviour to the Jade Emperor. The family leaves special food in front of the Kitchen God's picture or statue before he goes. These are sweet sticky foods so that he gives a 'sweet' report of the family's behaviour. Some people say the sticky food is to stick his mouth shut so he cannot open it to tell the Jade Emperor anything bad! The picture of the old Kitchen God is burnt (to symbolize his departure) or turned to face the wall. The new picture is welcomed with more offerings of food on New Year's Eve.

This traditional picture of the Kitchen God, his wife and children gives important dates at the top, as well as the year (1996). The dates of his departure and return are given at the side of the picture.

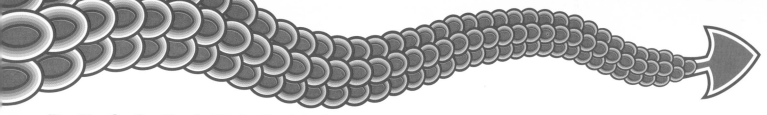

DECORATIONS

Pictures – wall posters – have a long tradition in China and are an important part of the New Year Festival. The Chinese decorate their homes with new pictures and papercuts with sayings inscribed in beautiful handwriting done with a brush (calligraphy) for the celebrations.

Most pictures have a lucky meaning because in Chinese many sounds have two meanings. The Chinese word for 'oranges' sounds the same as the word for 'gold' and also for 'auspicious' (lucky), so oranges are shown in pictures for wealth and luck.

The Chinese word for 'fish' sounds the same as the word for 'surplus', so pictures of children holding fishes (meaning a wish for lots of children) are common.

Wood block prints like this one have a long history. At New Year they express a wish for peace and good fortune in the year to come.

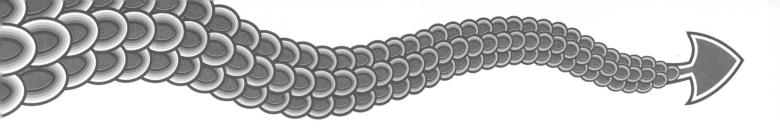

Pasting up verses on red paper about the New Year is common throughout Chinese communities. These offer good wishes to all passers by and especially anyone crossing the threshold. People in China like to think up their own 'spring couplets' to paste up on their door.

SPRING COUPLETS

As well as lucky pictures there is a tradition of pasting up pairs of sayings (spring couplets) that offer good wishes at the beginning of the New Year. These are usually painted on red paper. These are some typical sayings:

Chu ru ping an
May you be blessed with peace and safety wherever you are
Si ji ping an
May you be blessed with peace and safety in all four seasons

May all your wishes come true
May your business prosper

Good luck and good fortune
Riches be with you if you live in harmony

Papercuts are a traditional decoration still used today. Coloured paper is cut in the shape of animals, children, flowers or one of several lucky Chinese characters. These are stuck on windows so that the light shines through them. Bright colours are considered lucky, especially red, which is the colour of wealth and happiness.

Traditional papercuts.

FOOD CUSTOMS

Food is very important to the Chinese. Each of their festivals has special foods associated with it, each food having a special meaning.

For example, on New Year's Eve, every family tries to have fish and to leave some over. This has the special double meaning – next year there will be fish to eat, and next year's harvest will be plentiful and more than enough. Many foods are considered lucky because the name of the food sounds like a word for wealth, long life, plenty, or children.

Jiaozi are dumplings made for special occasions in the north of China. They are often made at home with the whole family involved in the preparation. They are eaten at midnight – at the end of the old year and the beginning of the new year.

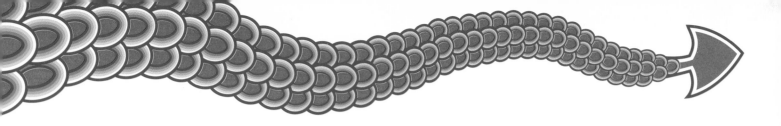

A favourite food at New Year from northern China, is jiaozi (dumplings). All over the world Chinese people enjoy making this traditional food. Making jiaozi is something the whole family helps with. The most common filling is pork mince with Chinese cabbage, flavoured with garlic, fresh coriander, ginger and soy sauce.

Other fillings are used for special meanings. For example, peanuts will bring long life, sugar will bring a sweet life, money will mean that one has money to spend. This is similar to the tradition of putting charms and sixpences in Christmas puddings.

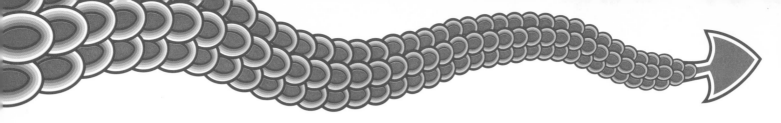

The main meal on New Year's Eve usually begins in the late afternoon. Dumplings are eaten at the beginning of the meal or as side dishes. Traditionally, most families would have meat for the main New Year feast, and make bean curd, sausages and special wine for the occasion. Vegetables (cabbage, turnips, dried mushrooms), pork, chicken and fish (for wealth, health and luck) are eaten with every imaginable flavouring. Special delicacies, such as sliced jellyfish, sea cucumbers, shark's fin and bird's nests (for wealthier families) and giant pork meat balls called 'Lion's heads' are all served in enormous quantities.

The New Year's Eve feast is the first of many grand meals in the days that follow. As friends and relatives arrive to celebrate the New Year, each day sees a banquet to honour the visitors. As they arrive, the guests will be greeted with many different snack foods: watermelon seeds, sesame sweets, preserved eggs, roasted peanuts, pears, oranges and special assorted cakes with good luck motives printed or moulded on to them.

Sweets are prepared to look especially inviting for guests at New Year.

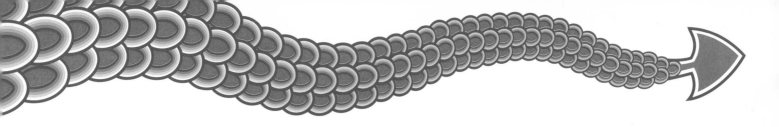

The food in Southern China for the New Year celebration differs from the North. The North has dumplings; in the South rice is ritually washed over several days. This is then called the 'grain for 10,000 years' (wan nian liang). It is eaten during the celebrations to bring good fortune. Another traditional food in the South is nian gao, or New Year's Cake, made with glutinous rice flour and sugar. The sounds 'nian gao' may also be understood to mean 'rising high year' and the stickiness is supposed to remind people of friendship and sticking together.

Above: This display of New Year specialities includes eight precious rice, rice pudding with cherries on top, noodles for long life, oranges for wealth and filled buns with good luck characters on them.

These young men selling fast food on the streets of Beijing have dressed up in red for the New Year.

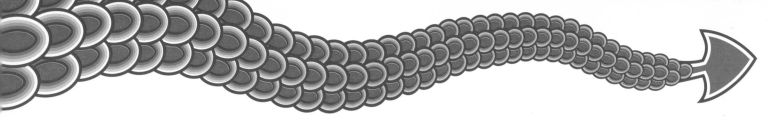

MUSIC, DANCE AND DRAMA

Dragon dances are the most spectacular dances performed at New Year. In ancient China the dragon was considered a friendly and helpful beast and was associated with longlife, good fortune and rain. The longer the dragon, the more good he will bring to the community, so the aim is to have a very long dragon with as many people carrying the dragon's tail as possible. There may be twenty or thirty people holding up the dragon's tail. (In Perth, Australia, the Chinese community is said to have the longest dragon in the world at 56.7 metres!)

The dragon's head is usually very elaborate and sometimes very large. It is believed to come alive when the eyes are painted in. This one, photographed in Washington DC, USA, appears to have eyes that actually light up.

MAKE A DRAGON

Make a dragon with a long tail for lots of children to dance under – better still make two dragons so that they can dance together.

Make the dragon's head using a large cardboard box painted in bright colours and with big eyes and ears and a large mouth for the 'head' person to see through. Make the body using old material painted with fluorescent pens.

One child holds the dragon's head and two or three (or more if you have lots of material and can make a long tail) children follow holding up the tail. The dragon can then snake its way around the classroom following a child who leads the dragon with a pearl (balloon or lantern) at the end of a stick.

This very long dragon is part of the New Year celebrations taking place in Turfan in northwest China.

The dragon follows a leader, who dances along ahead of the dragon carrying a lantern or a 'pearl' on a stick. If there is more than one dragon there may be a competition to see which dragon can run and dance for the longest.

The dragon may also try and catch money offered by spectators. The higher the money is held the greater the amount, though it is bad luck to hold the money out of reach. The performers may stand on one another's shoulders to 'climb walls' for money offered from an upstairs window.

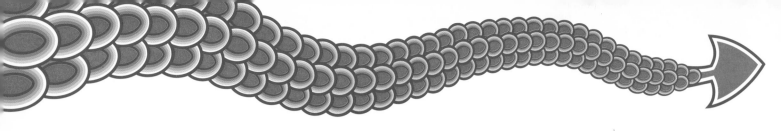

In London's Chinatown, the New Year is celebrated on the first Sunday of the New Year with street celebrations and a Lion Dance. Green leaves and packets of money are hung on shopfronts and are fed to the dancing lion. Firecrackers are also hung up, ready to be set off when the lion visits. The more noise, the greater the number of bad spirits that are chased away.

Lion dancing is a traditional folk sport in which groups of players dress up and tour the villages and perform set dances. Lions are supposed to bring good fortune but real lions are not found in China. It is thought that the idea comes from the Tibetan dog motif. The head is domed with bulging, lidded eyes which open and close, and a curly, colourful mane. The body is decorated with tassels and little bells.

Each lion is operated by two men. The head is carried by one dancer, who rears up and crouches down while another, carrying the body, carefully mimics his moves. While the lion dances to the accompaniment of gongs and drums, more dancers, two dressed as monkeys and two as clowns, may entertain the audience with acrobatics and by pulling faces. Lion dances have a long history, and the dancers are often very skilful at performing stunts and dancing.

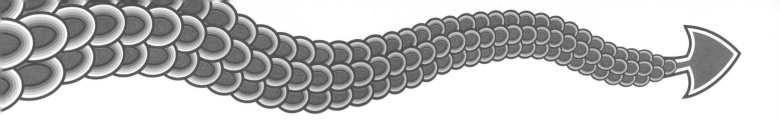

In the countryside in south China the drum and gong contests are grand events and the sound of drums and gongs may be heard from the New Year right up to the fifteenth day. Every village sends a team of a drum, cymbals and several gongs to a local fair and the contest forms part of wide-scale recreational activities. The drummer acts as the conductor and the other instruments perform in time to his beat. As the drummer gets faster, the ensemble gets faster and louder, with everyone beating their own instrument as loudly as possible. This can be excitingly noisy in the otherwise peaceful countryside.

This lion, pictured in London's Soho, is taking a rest. Behind it the dragon's head is rearing up out of the crowd.

NEW YEAR OPERA

Performing operas is an important part of the New Year's festivities. There are regional opera styles belonging to the different provinces in China. The best-known style is that performed in Beijing and Canton, but every area has its own local stories and styles of performance. The opera in the picture is being performed out of doors in a town in the Guizhou province.

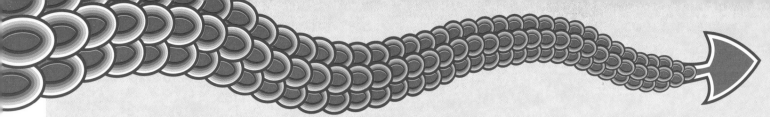

THE CHINESE CALENDAR

New Year's Eve
This is a time of preparation and for eating a big family meal. It is the day when the Kitchen God is welcomed back. Red envelopes containing money are given to children in the immediate family.

Welcoming the New Year
Children and adults stay up all night to welcome the New Year. Firecrackers are set off after midnight. This is followed by fifteen days of celebration.

Day 1: Chicken's Day (New Year's Day.) This is the day for worshipping ancestors and gods, visiting close relatives and giving and receiving red envelopes (from less immediate family).

Day 2: Dog's Day. More visits to relatives and friends are made.

Day 3: Sheep's Day. Also Squabble Day – not a day to see friends and relatives. On this day people visit the Buddhist temples.

Day 4: Pig's Day. The day when married daughters visit their parents.

Day 5: Ox's Day (Day of the God of Wealth). On this day taboos end. All the rubbish may be thrown out without fear of throwing away good luck or wealth.

Day 6: Horse's Day. Businesses re-open.

Day 7: Man's Day. Traditionally everyone gains a year in age on this day.

Day 8: Grain day. All the stars come down to earth on this day, which is set aside to welcome them in the Daoist temples.

Day 9: The Jade Emperor's birthday. Sacrifices are made to Heaven in the Daoist temples.

Days 10–14: Preparations for:

Day 15: The Lantern Festival. As well as Dragon and Lion dances, there may be parades of traditional costumes, acrobatics, operas, stilt performances and the waist drum dance. At night, people visit displays of lanterns. ▼

Qingming (Pure Brightness) **Festival** (about 3 or 4 April)
A day for visiting and sweeping graves. This is a rare Solar festival and is a thanksgiving for the return of the Sun and warmer weather; a time for honouring the dead and making offerings at the graves of relatives. Food, paper money and paper clothing are left for the afterlife.

▲ **Dragon Boat Festival** (5th day of fifth month)
This festival centres on the legend of Qu Yuan, a famous poet and political figure in the fourth century BC who threw himself into a lake as a political protest. Boats raced out to save his body from being eaten by the water-dragons by throwing rice balls into the water. Steamed rice balls wrapped in bamboo leaves are the speciality for this festival. Dragon Boat races are traditionally held at this time.

Mid Autumn Festival (15th day of eighth month)
A joyous occasion when the harvest moon is at its brightest. A time of thanksgiving and family reunion.

Mooncakes, the round cakes with ▲ sweet paste centres, are sold at this time. The cakes have a special significance, recalling the uprising against the Mongol invaders in the fourteenth century. Messages were sent secretly to the troops and sympathizers hidden inside mooncakes. In this way the rebellion was co-ordinated and the invaders defeated.

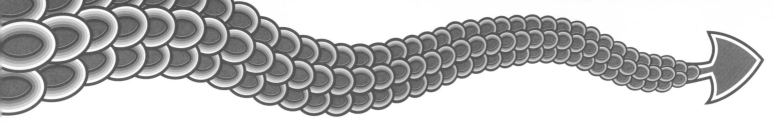

GLOSSARY

Ancestors Relatives from previous generations who have died.

Arrogant Proud, with a high opinion of your own importance.

Banquets Feasts.

Calligraphy An art form practised with a brush by nearly everyone in China. A good 'hand' takes many years to perfect.

Compassionate Friendly and co-operative, sympathetic.

Coriander A herb used in Chinese cooking. It is strong tasting and looks a bit like parsley.

Earthly desires The needs and wants of human beings, such as material goods.

Emperor A ruler of many countries.

Glutinous Sticky; late crops of cereals, especially rice, have more starch and are stickier than early crops.

Hoard To store something for future use.

Immortals In Chinese folk-lore there are eight 'immortals' – god-like beings with exceptional powers.

Incense A substance burned for its odour.

Lavish Generous or excessive, 'over the top'.

Longevity Long life.

Lunar Of the Moon.

New Moon When the Moon is not visible from the Earth. Opposite of a full moon.

Orbit The fixed course of a satellite or planet.

Prosperity Being wealthy and successful.

Solar Of the Sun.

Soul Spiritual part of a body believed to survive after death.

Symbolize To show something using signs or pictures.

Taboos Things that can or cannot be done because of a ritual or belief.

Tradition The ways things have been done for many hundreds of years.

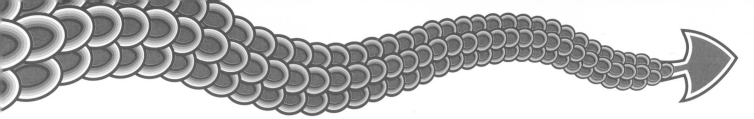

BOOKS TO READ

The Chinese in Britain by Anthony Shang (Batsford Academic and Educational, London, 1984)

Chinese Migrations by Judith Kendra (Wayland Publishers, 1994)

Festival! Chinese New Year by Olivia Bennett (Macmillan Education, London, 1986)

BOOKS FOR TEACHERS

Festival! Chinese New Year –Teacher's Notes and Pupils' Worksheets by Rosalind Kerven (Macmillan Education, London, 1986).

Folk Customs at Traditional Chinese Festivities by Qi Xing (Foreign Languages Press, Beijing, 1988).

Dragon Boat – 20 Chinese Folksongs for Voices and Instruments by Gaik See Chew (Chester Music, London, 1986).
A wonderful collection of songs suitable for children, with tuned and untuned instrument accompaniment.

Festivals by John Gilbert (OUP Music Dept, 1986).
The chapter on Chinese New Year includes background information, activities and songs. Covers all major world festivals and their associated music and musical references.

USEFUL INFORMATION

The Commonwealth Institute, Kensington High Street, London, W8 6NR.
(Organizes lectures, seminars and courses for teachers. Runs an annual course on the Chinese New Year Festival for Primary Schools.)

Great Britain China Centre, 15 Belgrave Square, London, SW1X 8PS.
(Publishes the magazine *China Review*. Good reference library on China.)

Chinese Community Centre, 2nd floor, 44 Gerard St, London, W1V 2LP.
(Publishes booklets on Chinese culture in English. Co-ordinates Chinese activities in central London.)

Lambeth Chinese Community Association, 69 Stockwell Road, London, SW9 9PY.
(Organizes cultural events and festivals.)

Victoria and Albert Museum (V&A), Exhibition Road, South Kensington, London.
(Organizes courses on Chinese culture. Has large exhibition of Chinese artefacts.)

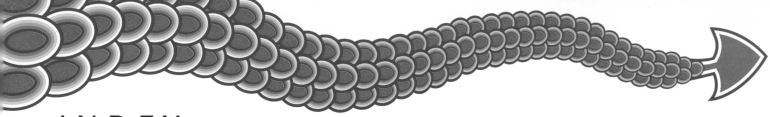

INDEX